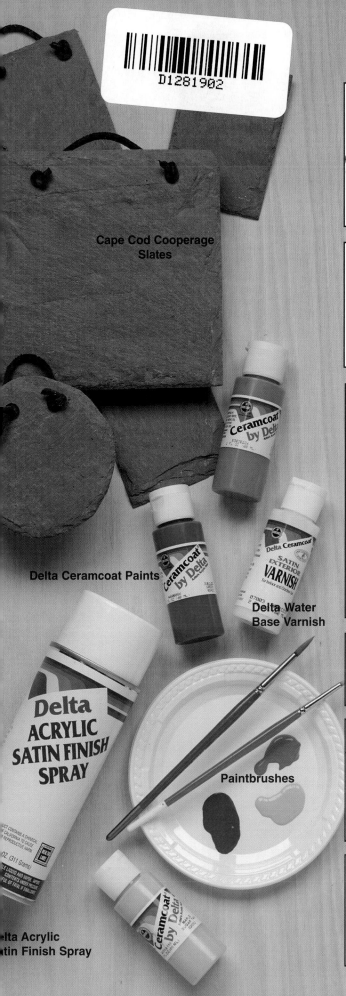

Cape Cod Cooperage Slates

Delta Ceramcoat Paints

Delta Water Base Varnish

Paintbrushes

Delta ACRYLIC SATIN FINISH SPRAY

Delta Acrylic Satin Finish Spray

Basic Tips & Instructions

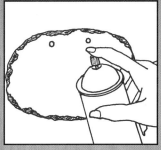

Slate. Remove leather hanger. Wash slate with detergent to remove dirt and any other small particles. Dry thoroughly. Spray slate with a light coat of Delta Acrylic Satin Finish.

Pattern. Trace pattern onto tracing paper. Tape pattern on slate with transfer paper between slate and pattern. Trace design lightly with a pen or stylus.

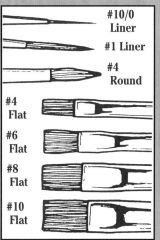

Paint project following the instructions for individual projects.
Use the size and style brush indicated for each area of each project. Refer to photo of project to shade and highlight details.
Use Delta Ceramcoat Acrylic paints.
Clean brushes with water.

Glue the wood pieces and other embellishments on slates with Delta Quik n' Tacky Glue.

Finish. Seal finished projects with Delta Ceramcoat Varnish, Delta Satin Finish Spray or Delta High Gloss Acrylic Finish Spray. Tie leather hanger on slate.

Color Float. To make floating and line work quicker and easier, add one drop of Color Float to one ounce of water before wetting brush.

Meet the Designers

Diane Bantz

Thanks to Diane, a versatile designer who loves to paint everything from florals to landscapes. A former shop owner and long time teacher, Diane instructs classes for other teachers of painting techniques.

Dorris Sorensen

Thanks to Dorris whose designs are delightful. Dorris paints to sell in her own boutique and teaches painting. Her designs are easy to paint and have a strong appeal for beginners in the painting field.

Shea A. Szachara

Thanks to Shea, the Director of Creative and Educational Services for Delta. She has been a member of the Delta Design Force since its inception and works in all designing areas.

Sharon Tittle

Thanks to Sharon for sharing her techniques. An award-winning designer, she has provided designs for businesses, schools, the entertainment field and non-profit organizations.

Barbie Vasek

Thanks to Barbie, who has won many awards in fabric painting. She is very active in her local painting chapter, teaches many classes, and produces her own line of hot-selling pattern packets.

Billie Worrell

Thanks to Billie for her designs. She currently owns a very successful teaching studio and is a former shop owner. An outstanding fabric painter, she is equally talented in all mediums.

'Birds Welcome' Plaque

FRONT COVER PHOTO   *by Sharon Tittle*

DELTA PRODUCTS:
Color Float
Quick n' Tacky glue
Navy Blue, Village Green, Liberty Blue, Crocus Yellow, Antique Gold, Red Iron Oxide, Woodland Night Green, Light Ivory and Autumn Brown Ceramcoat Paints
Ceramcoat Satin Exterior Varnish
MATERIALS:
Cape Cod Cooperage 8" x 10" Tombstone slate
Tall Burgundy/Green, short Gold/Green and Blue/Burgundy wood birdhouses with wire hangers
10 assorted $\frac{1}{8}$", $\frac{1}{4}$" and $\frac{1}{2}$" buttons
Heart and flower buttons
Light Brown silk ribbon rose
#6 shader and #4 liner brushes
Black fine tip permanent marking pen
INSTRUCTIONS:
1. Trace pattern and transfer onto slate.
2. Using Color Float, side load brush with Woodland Night Green and Village Green to paint letters. Add Red Iron Oxide highlight stripes.
3. For bird body, mix 1 part Red Iron Oxide and 2 parts Woodland Night Green. Paint hair and beak Antique Gold. Dot eyes with Light Ivory, add Autumn Brown dot. Dry brush wings with Antique Gold. Add outlines and details with pen.
4. Float cats with Autumn Brown and Antique Gold. Side load colors. Paint mouths and noses Antique Gold, highlight noses with Autumn Brown. Dot eyes Light Ivory, add Autumn Brown dot. Add details and outlines with pen.
5. Paint tree trunks Autumn Brown. Outline and add wood lines with Black pen.
6. Double load and float flowers Navy Blue with Crocus Yellow, Red Iron Oxide with Crocus Yellow and Red Iron Oxide with Light Ivory as desired. Use Woodland Night Green and Village Green to float leaves. Outline petals and leaves, draw stems with Black pen.
7. Glue birdhouses in place.
8. On tall birdhouse, paint squares Village Green with Woodland Night Green lines. Paint vines Village Green and leaves Woodland Night Green. Add squiggles with pen.
9. On center birdhouse, paint stars Liberty Blue. Add Navy Blue dots and Red Iron Oxide lines. Outline stars with pen.
10. On remaining birdhouse, paint flower petals Red Iron Oxide, dot centers Crocus Yellow. Paint bottom heart Red Iron Oxide, add Antique Gold dots. Paint chimney bricks Red Iron Oxide. Add smoke using Antique Gold and Crocus Yellow. Outline heart and chimney with Black pen. Draw accents on smoke with pen.
11. Seal plaque and birdhouses with varnish.
12. Referring to photo for placement, glue buttons and rose in place. Replace leather hanger.

Watermelon 'Mom's Cafe' Sign

FRONT COVER PHOTO

by Dorris Sorensen

DELTA PRODUCTS:

Bright Red, Tangerine, Black Cherry, Seminole Green,
   Woodland Night Green, Crocus Yellow, Empire Gold,
   White, Terra Cotta, Dark Brown and Black Ceramcoat Paints

Acrylic High Gloss Finish Spray

MATERIALS:

Cape Cod Cooperage 7" round slate

Black fabric marker

½" x 1" piece of artificial sponge

#10 and #6 flat and #1 scroller brushes

INSTRUCTIONS:

1. Prepare slate as instructed in Basic Tips on page 3.
2. Paint center of melon Bright Red following natural contour of edge. Leave chipped edges showing. While still wet, slip-slap Tangerine on lower portion and Black Cherry on upper portion.
3. Trace and transfer pattern.
4. Paint rind Seminole Green around top and side of slate as shown in photo. Sponge stripes with Woodland Night Green.
5. Add White letters, using scroller brush.
6. Load #10 flat brush with Empire Gold, side load Crocus Yellow. Stroke sunflower petals and buds with Crocus on outside edge. Work from outer edge to center of flowers.
7. Double load #6 flat brush with Woodland Night Green and Seminole Green to stroke leaves.
8. For bud bases, double load #1 scroller with Woodland Night Green and Seminole Green.
9. Use Dark Brown for flower center, shade bottom Black. When dry, float Terra Cotta around edge with #10 flat brush.
10. Use #1 scroller with Black for seeds, dot White highlights.
11. Add lines with Black marker.
12. Spray with finish. Replace leather hanger.

Angelic Flower Maiden

FRONT COVER PHOTO   *by Barbie Vasek*

DELTA PRODUCTS:
Color Float
Ceramcoat Sparkle Glaze
Light Ivory, Barn Red, Charcoal, Maple Sugar Tan,
    Seminole Green, Santa's Flesh, Adobe Red,
    Denim Blue and Antique Gold Ceramcoat Paints
Ceramcoat Satin Exterior Varnish
MATERIALS:
Cape Cod Cooperage 6" x 10" rectangle slate
Sponge
Black fine tip permanent marker
#4 pointed round, #6 flat and liner brushes
INSTRUCTIONS:
1. Prepare slate. Sponge a light coat of Light Ivory on slate front, leaving edges unpainted.
2. Trace and transfer pattern.
3. Use round brush to basecoat face, hands and feet with Santa's Flesh. Add a touch of Barn Red to the brush and lightly blush cheeks. Dot eyes Charcoal, add a tiny Light Ivory highlight dot.
4. Basecoat wings with Light Ivory. While paint is still wet, add feather strokes of Denim Blue, using round brush. Start strokes at base of wing and pull toward tip.
5. Basecoat sleeve and hem edge of dress Denim Blue. Basecoat dress top Adobe Red. Let dry.
6. To accent sleeve, dry brush Light Ivory over Denim Blue, Pull strokes toward cuff. Add taps of Light Ivory to cuff for lace.
7. Paint hearts on hem edge Maple Sugar Tan.
8. Make large Denim Blue dots at bottom of Red dress.
9. Add a Barn Red squiggle line above dots with a Light Ivory highlight. Make graduated dots above line with Antique Gold.
10. Basecoat each flower Antique Gold, add Light Ivory centers. Make Seminole Green leaves and stems.
11. Hair is created with light taps of Maple Sugar Tan and Antique Gold that run together. Add Light Ivory taps for highlights.
12. Lightly paint halo Antique Gold, using liner brush.
13. When paint dries, use pen to outline each shape of design. Outline hearts at hem, shade one edge of dots at hem. Dash lines along bottom of squiggle, shade one side of dots above line. Make gather lines from cuff on sleeves. Add squiggle curls to hair. Lightly suggest feathers on wings. Add lines on each flower petal. Make a line down the center of leaves, shade one side of stems.
14. Seal with varnish. When dry, coat wings with Sparkle Glaze.
15. Seal with varnish again. Replace leather hanger.

Lake Michigan Lighthouse

PAGE 10-11 PHOTO   *by Diane Bantz*

DELTA PRODUCTS:

Mallard Green, Denim Blue, Black, Barn Red, Burnt Umber, Nightfall Blue, White and Oyster White Ceramcoat Paints
Ceramcoat Satin Exterior Varnish

MATERIALS:

Cape Cod Cooperage 7" round slate
#4 and #8 flat, #1 liner and fan brushes

INSTRUCTIONS:

1. Prepare slate. Trace and transfer pattern.
2. Mix Denim Blue and White + a little Black for sky. Start at top and work down to horizon, adding more White as you paint. Go around cloud area.
3. For clouds, use a clean brush to pick up White. Push up on brush, allowing color to come off end of brush. Pick up a little Denim Blue near horizon. Add more Denim Blue to shade between clouds.
4. For the misty line of background trees at the center of the pattern, pick up White + Black on #4 flat brush. With the chisel edge of brush, pat on slate to make small vertical lines. Do not overwork .
5. Repeat technique for foreground trees, picking up Mallard Green + Denim Blue + Black, keeping darkest color at bottom.
6. To create background water, brush streaks of Mallard + White, Denim Blue, White and Mallard Green + Black. Tap White across water with chisel edge of brush to create waves.
7. Basecoat lighthouse and building Oyster White. Float Nightfall Blue then Black to shade left sides. Add shade above building roof, at corner of building and to lighthouse at right edge of building. Paint roofs Barn Red with Oyster White highlights on right side. Use thinned Black with liner brush to outline glass panes and for catwalk rail. Highlight railing with White. Make slashes of Black + White then White across glass for a reflection. Paint windows on buildings Black. Paint birds Black.
8. Paint rock area with splotches of Burnt Umber, picking up Black for darker areas. Add Burnt Umber + White for light areas. Highlight with White.
9. For waves, brush on Mallard Green, Mallard Green + Denim Blue + Black and Nightfall Blue, keeping darkest colors toward front. Use fan brush and White to create foam. Tap end of brush for spray.
10. Seal with varnish. Replace hanger.

Hatteris Lighthouse

PAGE 10-11 PHOTO   *by Shea A. Szachara*

DELTA PRODUCTS:
Driftwood Color Accent Spray
Ceramcoat Crackle Medium
Silver Renaissance Foil and Foil Adhesive
Quick n' Tacky glue
White, Black, Bright Red and Drizzle Grey Ceramcoat Paints

MATERIALS:
Cape Cod Cooperage 2¾" x 12" slate
6" x 18" wood sign board (Walnut Hollow No.14072)
#4, #6 and #14 flat and #10/0 liner brushes
Black fine tip permanent marking pen
Sawtooth hanger, Hammer

INSTRUCTIONS:
1. Spray all surfaces of sign board with Driftwood. Let dry. Paint shaped edges of board Black. Use #14 brush to dampen edges of front of board with water. Float with Black to shade, allowing color to bleed into dampened area. Let dry thoroughly. Apply Crackle Medium along Black edges, allow to dry to tacky stage. Paint over crackled area with Drizzle Grey with a slip slap motion. Do not get medium or paint on front of board.
2. Prepare slate. Trace pattern and transfer outline of lighthouse.
3. Basecoat lighthouse shape with White. Let dry. Transfer stripes and pattern details. Paint diagonal stripes, top rim and rail Black. Paint three narrow horizontal stripes and roof Bright Red.
4. Following manufacturer's instructions, apply foil adhesive to area between roof and top Red stripe. When adhesive is clear, firmly press foil over area with dull side down. Draw lines for window panes with Black pen.
5. To shade lighthouse and define rocks, float Black down right side of lighthouse, along base and behind rocks. Float White down left side of lighthouse. Float Drizzle Grey over top edge of rocks. Float White highlights randomly on rocks. Float Black behind rocks.
6. Apply a generous amount of glue to back of slate, press in place on board. Weight if necessary until dry. Let glue dry completely. Attach hanger to board.

Heart of Spring Plaque

PAGE 14 PHOTO *by Sharon Tittle*

DELTA PRODUCTS:
Color Float
Quick n' Tacky glue
Autumn Brown, Crocus Yellow and Desert Sun Orange
  Ceramcoat Paints
Ceramcoat Satin Exterior Varnish

MATERIALS:
Cape Cod Cooperage Small heart slate
$1\frac{1}{2}$" whittled wood heart
Miniature ladybug and frog
2 Yellow and 3 Blue silk flowers on wire stems
#2 flat and #1 liner brushes
Black fine tip permanent marking pen

INSTRUCTIONS:
1. Prepare slate. Trace pattern and transfer to slate.
2. Using Color Float, side load brush Autumn Brown and Crocus Yellow. Paint letters.
3. Paint upper wings of butterfly Autumn Brown. Paint head, body, dots and lower wings Crocus Yellow.
5. With Black pen outline letters, add details and outlines on butterfly.
6 Paint heart Crocus Yellow, float edge Desert Sun Orange. Add squiggle line design and circles with pen.
7. Referring to photo, glue heart on slate. Bend flower stems in a curve, glue to upper edges of slate. Glue lady bug on flower stem and frog on slate.
8. Seal slate with varnish. Replace leather hanger.

'Welcome To The Lake' Plaque

PAGE 14 PHOTO

by Sharon Tittle

DELTA PRODUCTS:
Quick n' Tacky glue
Spice Brown, Maple Sugar Tan and Western Sunset Yellow
 Ceramcoat Paints

MATERIALS:
Cape Cod Cooperage 3" x 12" slate
Two 12" twigs
2 miniature lady bugs
Large feather butterfly, Grasshopper
Spanish moss
4 rubber bands
#6 shader and #1 liner brushes
Black fine tip permanent marking pen

INSTRUCTIONS:
1. Prepare slate. Trace pattern and transfer to slate.
2. Float letters Spice Brown and Maple Sugar Tan. Highlight with Western Sunset Yellow. Outline letters and draw wood marks with Black pen. Let dry.
3. Bend and glue twigs in the shape of a fish. Place fish on slate and hold in place with rubber bands. Squirt glue under twigs, let dry.
4. Paint Western Sunset Yellow squiggle line above fish.
5. Spray plaque with finish. Replace leather hanger.
6. Referring to photo, glue Spanish moss, butterfly, lady bugs and grasshopper on slate.
7. Optional: Feel free to add old fishing flies, lures or hooks to personalize your plaque and to make an excellent gift for your favorite bait caster. (Just make certain the lures are *old* ones, and not his current favorites!)

'Old Time Friendship' Slate

PAGE 14 PHOTO
by Sharon Tittle

DELTA PRODUCTS:
Color Float
Quick n' Tacky glue
Black Cherry and Old Parchment Ceramcoat Paints

MATERIALS:
Cape Cod Cooperage 6" x 8" oval slate
7 driftwood pieces
Acorn
Twelve 6mm wiggle eyes
#6 shader brush
Black fine tip permanent marking pen

INSTRUCTIONS:
1. Prepare slate. Trace and transfer pattern.
2. Using Color Float, side load brush and paint letters Old Parchment and Black Cherry. When dry, outline letters with Black pen.
3. Referring to photo, glue driftwood and acorn on slate.
4. Spray with finish. When dry, glue eyes in place. Replace leather hanger.

'Welcome' Plaque with Flowers

BACK COVER PHOTO

by Diane Bantz

DELTA PRODUCTS:

Acry-Blend™ Drying Retarder

Lilac Dusk, Denim Blue, Periwinkle Blue, Nightfall Blue, White, Vibrant Green, Crocus Yellow and Burnt Umber Ceramcoat Paints

'Welcome' Stencil Magic stencil

Stencil Adhesive Spray

Ceramcoat Satin Exterior Varnish

MATERIALS:

Cape Cod Cooperage 6" x 10" slate

Small irregularly torn sponge

#6 flat, #4 round and #1 liner brushes

INSTRUCTIONS:

1. Prepare slate according to Basic Tips on page 3.

2. Use a damp sponge to apply Lilac Dusk, White, Denim Blue and Periwinkle Blue to cover slate. Make edge darker. Allow to dry.

3. Sponge stencil 'Welcome' with Denim and Nightfall Blues.

4. With a little Acry-Blend on sponge, make Denim Blue, Periwinkle Blue and Lilac Dusk triangle patches using the picture as a guide. This forms the underneath shading of the flowers. The darkest color should be to the bottom of the triangle and the lightest at the top, or outer edge.

5. While paint is still damp, use round brush to create White, White and Lilac Dusk, White and Denim Blue, and White and Periwinkle Blue petals. To make petals, press and lift brush for each petal. Dot centers with Crocus Yellow. Dot lilacs at end of bouquet with brush, using Denim and Nightfall Blues. Add White dot highlights with tip of brush handle. (There are 4 petals per flower.)

6. Use Vibrant Green to add indistinct leaves and stems. Shade with Burnt Umber.

7. Float Nightfall Blue along right edges of letters. Repeat around flowers if more shading is needed.

8. Seal with varnish. Replace leather hanger.

'Welcome' Sign

BACK COVER PHOTO

by Barbie Vasek

DELTA PRODUCTS:

Color Float

Light Ivory, Bouquet Pink, Green Sea, Norsk Blue, White, Rosetta Pink and Tidal Pool Blue Ceramcoat Paints

Ceramcoat Satin Exterior Varnish

MATERIALS:

Cape Cod Cooperage 3" x 12" slate

Sponge

Black fine tip permanent marker

#4 pointed round, #4 flat and liner brushes

INSTRUCTIONS:

1. Prepare slate. Sponge front with a light coat of Light Ivory. Leave edges unpainted as shown in photo.

2. Trace and transfer pattern. Center design side to side and place bottom 'E' 1" above bottom of slate. Paint letters as follows:

W - basecoat Norsk Blue, add Rosetta Pink dots.

E - basecoat Bouquet Pink, add crosshatched lines of Norsk Blue and Light Ivory.

L - basecoat Green Sea, add small Bouquet Pink hearts.

C - basecoat Tide Pool Blue, add small dot Bouquet Pink flowers with White dot centers.

O - basecoat Rosetta Pink, add crosshatched Bouquet Pink and Light Ivory lines.

M - basecoat Bouquet Pink, add White flowers and Green Sea leaves.

E - basecoat Norsk Blue, add dot Light Ivory flowers with Rosetta Pink centers.

3. Add Color Float to water. Using corner of flat brush, float Tide Pool Blue around each letter, leaving $1/4$" of Light Ivory showing between letters and floated color. Let dry. Add stitches around Light Ivory edges with Black pen.

4. Seal slate with varnish. Replace leather hanger.

'An Apple for Teacher' Slate

PAGE 14 PHOTO   *by Dorris Sorensen*

DELTA PRODUCTS:
Ceramcoat Crackle Medium
White, Nightfall Blue, Tompte Red, Black Cherry, Antique
    Gold, Woodland Night Green, Seminole Green, Dark Brown
    and Black Ceramcoat Paints
Acrylic High Gloss Finish Spray

MATERIALS:
Cape Cod Cooperage 6" x 8" slate
#1 scroller and #10 flat brushes

INSTRUCTIONS:
1. Prepare slate as instructed in Basic Tips on page 3.

2. Apply a generous coat of Crackle Medium to slate. Follow the natural contour of the front, leaving chipped edges showing. Let dry until tacky (about 20 minutes). Do not dry completely.
3. Using #10 flat brush, apply a coat of White paint over crackled area. Do not overstroke. Let dry.
4. Trace and transfer pattern.
5. Basecoat apples with 2 or 3 coats of Tompte Red. Shade left sides with Black Cherry. When dry, scuff Antique Gold highlights, using a dry brush.
6. Use #10 brush double loaded with Seminole Green and Woodland Night Green to paint leaves.
7. Paint letters Nightfall Blue, using #1 scroller.
8. Use #1 scroller with thinned Black paint to do line work.
9. Spray with finish. Replace leather hanger.

'God Bless America'

PAGE 10-11 PHOTO   *by Billie Worrell*

DELTA PRODUCTS:

Color Float

Liberty Blue, Light Ivory and Mendocino Red
    Ceramcoat Paints

Snow White, Yellow Ochre and Royal Blue Stencil Paint Cremes

'God Bless America' Stencil Magic stencil

Stencil Adhesive Spray

High Gloss Finish Spray

MATERIALS:

Cape Cod Cooperage slates: Star, small oval and 4" circle

Natural raffia

Black fine tip permanent marking pen

Two 3/8" stencil and #1 and #10 flat brushes

INSTRUCTIONS:

1. Prepare slates as instructed in Basic Tips on page 3.

2. Basecoat star with Light Ivory. Mark 3/4" wide stripes as shown in photo. Paint alternating stripes with Mendocino Red. Using Color Float, float Liberty Blue at each edge of Light Ivory stripes.

3. Basecoat oval slate Light Ivory. Float edges with Liberty Blue.

4. Basecoat round slate Liberty Blue. Float edges with Light Ivory.

5. Lightly mist back of stencil with adhesive. Referring to photo, place stencils on slates.

6. Stencil all letters Snow White, let dry. Overcoat 'God' and 'America' with Royal Blue. Stencil stars Yellow Ochre.

7. When stencils are dry, outline with Black pen.

8. Spray with finish. Replace leather hangers. Tie raffia bow, glue on round slate hanger.

'Bath 5¢' Plaque

BACK COVER PHOTO   *by Barbie Vasek*

DELTA PRODUCTS:

Color Float

Light Ivory, Tide Pool Blue, Seminole Green, Adriatic Blue,
    Sachet Pink, Wild Rose and Kim Gold Ceramcoat Paints

Ceramcoat Satin Exterior Varnish

MATERIALS:

Cape Cod Cooperage 6" x 8" oval slate

Sponge, #4 pointed round, #4 flat and liner brushes

INSTRUCTIONS:

1. Prepare slate according to Basic Tips on page 3.

2. Sponge top of slate with a light coat of Light Ivory. Follow contour of slate front, leaving edges unpainted.

2. Trace and transfer pattern.

3. Basecoat lettering Adriatic Blue. When dry, add Kim Gold strokes, then make thinner strokes of Light Ivory over Kim Gold strokes for highlights.

4. Very lightly sponge Seminole Green background for roses.

5. For roses, basecoat ovals of Wild Rose. Add loose strokes of Sachet Pink and Light Ivory with liner brush.

6. Basecoat leaves loosely with Seminole Green. Shade with Wild Rose. Highlight with narrow strokes of Light Ivory.

7 Seal with varnish. Replace leather hanger.

Mom's Bake Shop

PAGE 18 PHOTO

DELTA PRODUCTS:

Yellow Ochre and Warm Brown Ceramcoat Stencil
    Paint Cremes

Antique White Ceramcoat Paint

String of Stars Stencil Magic stencil

Gingerbread Border Stencil Magic stencil

Stencil Adhesive Spray

Ceramcoat Satin Exterior Varnish

MATERIALS:

Cape Cod Cooperage 6" x 8" oval slate

Fine and large tip Black paint pens

Flat and stencil brushes

INSTRUCTIONS:

1. Prepare slate. Paint slate Antique White. Let dry thoroughly.

2. Lightly mist back of stencils with adhesive. Referring to photo, place stencils on slate. Stencil gingerbread man Warm Brown, keeping color darker at edges. Stencil stars solid Yellow Ochre.

3. Trace and transfer lettering to slate. Use large pen for 'Mom's Bake Shop'. Use fine pen for remaining letters, eyes and lines.

4. Use stencil brush and Warm Brown to lightly color slate edges.

5. Seal with varnish. Replace leather hanger.

Watermelon Plaque

PAGE 18 PHOTO   *by Diane Bantz*

DELTA PRODUCTS:
Color Float
Ceramcoat Crackle Medium
Hunter Green, Vibrant Green, White, Bright Red, Black,
    and Light Ivory Ceramcoat Paints
Copper Renaissance Foil and Foil Adhesive
Ceramcoat Satin Exterior Varnish
MATERIALS:
Cape Cod Cooperage 6" x 8" half round slate
#1 liner and #6 flat brushes
INSTRUCTIONS:
1. Prepare slate. Paint slate Hunter Green.
2. Apply an even coat of Crackle Medium, following the natural contour of the slate. Leave the edge Hunter Green. Let dry until tacky (about 20 minutes). Apply an even coat of Light Ivory. Do not overbrush. Let dry.
3. Trace and transfer pattern.
4. Paint '25¢' Hunter Green.
5. Basecoat watermelon and rind of slice with a mix of Hunter Green and Vibrant Green. Mix colors with brush. To shade, float Hunter Green then Hunter Green mixed with a little Black along bottom edges. Paint stripes on watermelon with a mix of Vibrant Green and White.
6. Add a White stripe above rind on slice. Stipple area above stripe with a mix of Bright Red and White, keeping color darker at bottom and almost White at top.
7. Add Black seed dots, dot tiny White highlights on seeds.
8. Brush foil adhesive on Hunter Green edge of slate, letters and price. Let adhesive dry until clear, apply foil. To accent letters, float Hunter Green at one side.
9. Seal with varnish. Replace leather hanger.

Don't Forget
to Stop
and Smell
the FLOWERS

25¢
Inside

DINE BANZ

Kitty's Playground

Mom's
Bake Shop
(always open)